ROYAL COURT

Royal Court Theatre presents

FACE TO THE WALL

by **Martin Crimp**

First performance at the Royal Court Jerwood Theatre Downstairs
Sloane Square, London on 12 March 2002.

FACE TO THE WALL

by **Martin Crimp**

Cast
Gillian Hanna
Paul Higgins
Sophie Okonedo
Peter Wight

Director **Katie Mitchell**
Lighting Designer **Paule Constable**
Sound Designer **Gareth Fry**
Artistic Consultant **Antoni Malinowski**
Casting Director **Lisa Makin**
Production Manager **Paul Handley**
Stage Manager **Pea Horsley**
Costume Supervisor **Iona Kenrick**
Company Voice Work **Patsy Rodenburg**

Royal Court Theatre would like to thank the following for their help with this production:
Southwark Playhouse, Wardrobe care by Persil and Comfort courtesy of Lever Fabergé.

THE COMPANY

Martin Crimp (writer)
For the Royal Court: The Country (2000), Attempts on Her Life (1997), The Treatment (1993, winner of the John Whiting Award), No One Sees the Video (1991).
Other plays include: The Misanthrope (1996, Young Vic), Getting Attention (1992, West Yorkshire Playhouse), Play with Repeats (1989), Dealing with Clair (1988), Four Attempted Acts (1996, Orange Tree).
Translations for the Royal Court: The Chairs (1997, co-production with Theatre de Complicite).
Other translations include: The Triumph of Love (1999, Almeida), The Maids (1999, Young Vic), Roberto Zucco (1997, RSC).
Resident Dramatist at the Royal Court, 1997.

Paule Constable (lighting designer)
For the Royal Court: Boy Gets Girl, Mountain Language/Ashes To Ashes, Presence, Credible Witness, The Country, Dublin Carol, The Weir, The Glory of Living.
Other theatre includes: The Seagull, Tales from Ovid, The Dispute, Uncle Vanya, Beckett Shorts, The Mysteries (RSC); The Villains' Opera, Darker Face of the Earth, Haroun and the Sea of Stories, The Caucasian Chalk Circle (RNT); Amadeus (West End, Broadway, Olivier nomination); Vagina Monologues (West End); The Servant (Lyric); More Grimms' Tales (Young Vic and New York); four productions for Theatre de Complicite including the Olivier-nominated Street of Crocodiles.
Opera includes: productions for the Royal Opera House, English National Opera, Welsh National Opera, Scottish Opera, Opera North, Glyndebourne, La Monnaie.

Gareth Fry (sound designer)
For the Royal Court: Redundant, Mountain Language/Ashes To Ashes, The Country.
Other theatre includes: Accrington Pals (Chichester); The Oresteia (RNT); Noise of Time, Mnemonic, The Street of Crocodiles (Theatre de Complicite); Wexford Trilogy (Oxford Stage Company).

Gillian Hanna
For the Royal Court: Fireface, Hot Fudge and Ice Cream, Stranger's House; Road (1994) and The Queen and I (with Out of Joint); East is East (with Tamasha/Theatre Royal Stratford East).
Other theatre includes: The Caucasian Chalk Circle, Braddock's Time (Everyman, Liverpool); Teen Dreams, Calamity Jane, Gentlemen Prefer Blondes, Kiss and Kill, Vinegar Tom, Scum: Death, Destruction and Dirty Washing, Origin of the Species (Monstrous Regiment); City Echoes, Sweeny Todd, Tale of Two Cities (Liverpool Playhouse); Sweeny Todd, Destiny, Spend Spend Spend, Elizabeth, Almost by Chance a Woman (Half Moon); Duet for One (Crucible); The House of Bernada Alba (Lyric Hammersmith); Curtains (Hampstead Theatre); Wuthering Heights, Who's Afraid of Virginia Woolf, A Common Woman, Leonce and Lena (Crucible, Sheffield); Juno and the Paycock (Contact, Manchester); Wallflowering (West Yorkshire Playhouse); Romeo and Juliet, A View From the Bridge (Royal Exchange); Big Maggie (Birmingham Rep); A Passionate Woman (Leicester Haymarket); Emma (Edinburgh Festival and Tricycle); Ariadne Auf Naxos (Edinburgh Festival Theatre); Medea (Queens).
Television includes: Brookside, Horizon, All Creatures Great and Small, Making News, Sweet Sixteen, The Roughest Way, House of Bernada Alba, Poirot, The Marshall, The Story of Phillip Knight, Desmonds, Brookside, Drop the Dead Donkey, The Heart Surgeon, Dangerfield, All the Queen's Men, Where the Heart Is.
Film includes: Wolves of Willoughby Chase, The Woman and the Wolf, Les Miserables, Best.

Paul Higgins
For the Royal Court: Conquest of the South Pole, American Bagpipes, A Wholly Healthy Glasgow (also Royal Exchange, Manchester).
Other theatre includes: The Birthday Party (Shared Experience); A View From the Bridge, Romeo and Juliet, The Odd Women, The Way of the World (Royal Exchange, Manchester); The Hare Trilogy, An Enemy of the People (RNT); The Lady From the Sea (Lyric Hammersmith and West Yorkshire Playhouse); Slab Boys Trilogy (Young Vic); The Maidenstone, Buried Alive (Hampstead); Macbeth (English Touring Co. and Lyric Hammersmith); Conversations After a Burial (Almeida).
Television includes: The Negotiator, A Wholly Healthy Glasgow, A Very Peculiar Practice, Tumbledown, Dr Finlay, Staying Alive, Beating Jesus, Murder.
Film includes: Bedrooms and Hallways, Complicity.
Writing for television: Opera Lovers and Peripheral Vision for the Series Table 12.

Katie Mitchell (director)
For the Royal Court: Nightsongs, Mountain Language/Ashes To Ashes, The Country.
Other theatre includes: A Woman Killed With Kindness, The Dybbuk, Ghosts, Henry VI, Easter, Phoenician Woman, The Mysteries, Beckett Shorts, Uncle Vanya (with The Young Vic) (RSC); Rutherford and Son, The Machine Wreckers, The Oresteia (RNT); Iphigenia at Aulis, The Last Ones (Abbey Dublin); Endgame (Donmar Warehouse); Attempts on Her Life (Piccolo Teatro di Milano); The Maids (Young Vic).
Opera includes: Don Giovanni, Jenufa and Katya Kabanova (Welsh National Opera).
Awards include: 1996 Evening Standard Award for Best Director for The Phoenician Woman (RSC).

Sophie Okonedo
For the Royal Court: I Just Stopped By To See The Man, Been So Long.
Other theatre includes: Troilus and Cressida, Money (RNT); Arabian Nights (Young Vic); His Lordship's Fancy (Gate); A Jovial Crew, The Odyssey, Tamburlaine the Great, The Changeling (RSC); 900 Oneonta (Old Vic).
Television includes: Never Never, Clocking Off, Sweet Revenge, Staying Alive, Deep Secrets, Maria's Child.
Film includes: This Year's Love, The Jackal, Go Now, Ace Ventura II, Miss Queencake, Dirty, Pretty Things.
Radio includes: Pocahontas, Richard III, Timbuktu.

Peter Wight
For the Royal Court: Mouth To Mouth (& Albery); Not A Game For Boys, Sudlow's Dawn.
Other theatre includes: Sleep With Me, Waiting for Godot, Black Snow, Arturo Ui, Murmuring Judges (RNT); Much Ado About Nothing, Spanish Tragedy, Hamlet, Clockwork Orange, Barbarians (RSC); Edward II (Royal Exchange, Manchester); A Passion in Six Days, Mystery Bouffe, The Nest, Midsummer Night's Dream, Joking Apart (Crucible, Sheffield); King Lear, Three Sisters (Birmingham Rep); The Nose, Hedda Gabler, Risky City (Belgrade, Coventry); Hard to Get (Traverse, Edinburgh); The Seagull, Chekov's Women (West End); Grace, Dearly Beloved (Hampstead); Othello, Commedia, A State of Affairs, Progress (Lyric Hammersmith); The Caretaker (Globe Theatre Company, Warsaw); The Seagull (Shared Experience); Julius Cesaer, Take One (Maison Bertaux).
Television includes: Midsomer Murders, Care, The Blind Date, Active Defence, Our Mutual Friend, Jane Eyre, Wokenwell, Staying Alive, Touch of Frost, The Passion, Out of the Blue, Devil's Advocate, Speaking in Tongues, Meat, Anna Lee, Hearts and Minds, Will You Still Love Me, Yesterday's Dreams, Codename Kyril, The Fourth Floor, Casualty, Exclusive Yarns, Return of The Native.
Film includes: The Gathering, Three Blind Mice, Lucky Break, The Fourth Angel, Shiner, Fairytale, Secret and Lies, Naked, Meantime, Personal Services, A Small Deposit, A Turnip Head's Guide to Alan Parker.

THE ENGLISH STAGE COMPANY AT THE ROYAL COURT

The English Stage Company at the Royal Court opened in 1956 as a subsidised theatre producing new British plays, international plays and some classical revivals.

The first artistic director George Devine aimed to create a writers' theatre, 'a place where the dramatist is acknowledged as the fundamental creative force in the theatre and where the play is more important than the actors, the director, the designer'. The urgent need was to find a contemporary style in which the play, the acting, direction and design are all combined. He believed that 'the battle will be a long one to continue to create the right conditions for writers to work in'.

Devine aimed to discover 'hard-hitting, uncompromising writers whose plays are stimulating, provocative and exciting'. The Royal Court production of John Osborne's Look Back in Anger in May 1956 is now seen as the decisive starting point of modern British drama and the policy created a new generation of British playwrights. The first wave included John Osborne, Arnold Wesker, John Arden, Ann Jellicoe, N F Simpson and Edward Bond. Early seasons included new international plays by Bertolt Brecht, Eugène Ionesco, Samuel Beckett, Jean-Paul Sartre and Marguerite Duras.

The theatre started with the 400-seat proscenium arch Theatre Downstairs, and then in 1969 opened a second theatre, the 60-seat studio Theatre Upstairs. Some productions transfer to the West End, such as Caryl Churchill's Far Away, Conor McPherson's The Weir, Kevin Elyot's Mouth to Mouth and My Night With Reg. The Royal Court also co-produces plays which have transferred to the West End or toured internationally, such as Sebastian Barry's The Steward of Christendom and Mark Ravenhill's Shopping and Fucking (with Out of Joint), Martin McDonagh's The Beauty Queen Of Leenane (with Druid Theatre Company), Ayub Khan-Din's East is East (with Tamasha Theatre Company, and now a feature film).

Since 1994 the Royal Court's artistic policy has again been vigorously directed to finding and producing a new generation of playwrights. The writers include Joe Penhall, Rebecca Prichard, Michael Wynne, Nick Grosso, Judy Upton, Meredith Oakes, Sarah Kane, Anthony Neilson, Judith Johnson, James Stock, Jez Butterworth, Marina Carr, Simon Block, Martin McDonagh, Mark Ravenhill, Ayub Khan-Din, Tamantha Hammerschlag, Jess Walters, Che Walker, Conor McPherson, Simon Stephens, Richard Bean, Roy

photo: Andy Chopping

Williams, Gary Mitchell, Mick Mahoney, Rebecca Gilman, Christopher Shinn, Kia Corthron, David Gieselmann, Marius von Mayenburg, David Eldridge, Leo Butler, Zinnie Harris, Grae Cleugh, Roland Schimmelpfennig and Vassily Sigarev. This expanded programme of new plays has been made possible through the support of A.S.K Theater Projects, the Jerwood Charitable Foundation, the American Friends of the Royal Court Theatre and many in association with the Royal National Theatre Studio.

In recent years there have been record-breaking productions at the box office, with capacity houses for Jez Butterworth's Mojo, Sebastian Barry's The Steward of Christendom, Martin McDonagh's The Beauty Queen of Leenane, Ayub Khan-Din's East is East, Eugène Ionesco's The Chairs, David Hare's My Zinc Bed and Conor McPherson's The Weir, which transferred to the West End in October 1998 and ran for nearly two years at the Duke of York's Theatre.

The newly refurbished theatre in Sloane Square opened in February 2000, with a policy still inspired by the first artistic director George Devine. The Royal Court is an international theatre for new plays and new playwrights, and the work shapes contemporary drama in Britain and overseas.

AWARDS FOR THE ROYAL COURT

Terry Johnson's Hysteria won the 1994 Olivier Award for Best Comedy, and also the Writers' Guild Award for Best West End Play. Kevin Elyot's My Night with Reg won the 1994 Writers' Guild Award for Best Fringe Play, the Evening Standard Award for Best Comedy, and the 1994 Olivier Award for Best Comedy. Joe Penhall was joint winner of the 1994 John Whiting Award for Some Voices. Sebastian Barry won the 1995 Writers' Guild Award for Best Fringe Play, the Critics' Circle Award and the 1995 Lloyds Private Banking Playwright of the Year Award for The Steward of Christendom. Jez Butterworth won the 1995 George Devine Award, the Writers' Guild New Writer of the Year Award, the Evening Standard Award for Most Promising Playwright and the Olivier Award for Best Comedy for Mojo.

The Royal Court was the overall winner of the 1995 Prudential Award for the Arts for creativity, excellence, innovation and accessibility. The Royal Court Theatre Upstairs won the 1995 Peter Brook Empty Space Award for innovation and excellence in theatre.

Michael Wynne won the 1996 Meyer-Whitworth Award for The Knocky. Martin McDonagh won the 1996 George Devine Award, the 1996 Writers' Guild Best Fringe Play Award, the 1996 Critics' Circle Award and the 1996 Evening Standard Award for Most Promising Playwright for The Beauty Queen of Leenane. Marina Carr won the 19th Susan Smith Blackburn Prize (1996/7) for Portia Coughlan. Conor McPherson won the 1997 George Devine Award, the 1997 Critics' Circle Award and the 1997 Evening Standard Award for Most Promising Playwright for The Weir. Ayub Khan-Din won the 1997 Writers' Guild Awards for Best West End Play and Writers' Guild New Writer of the Year and the 1996 John Whiting Award for East is East (co-production with Tamasha).

At the 1998 Tony Awards, Martin McDonagh's The Beauty Queen of Leenane (co-production with Druid Theatre Company) won four awards including Garry Hynes for Best Director and was nominated for a further two. Eugene Ionesco's The Chairs (co-production with Theatre de Complicite) was nominated for six Tony awards. David Hare won the 1998 Time Out Live Award for Outstanding Achievement and six awards in New York including the Drama League, Drama Desk and New York Critics Circle Award for Via Dolorosa. Sarah Kane won the 1998 Arts Foundation Fellowship in Playwriting. Rebecca Prichard won the 1998 Critics' Circle Award for Most Promising Playwright for Yard Gal (co-production with Clean Break).

Conor McPherson won the 1999 Olivier Award for Best New Play for The Weir. The Royal Court won the 1999 ITI Award for Excellence in International Theatre. Sarah Kane's Cleansed was judged Best Foreign Language Play in 1999 by Theater Heute in Germany. Gary Mitchell won the 1999 Pearson Best Play Award for Trust. Rebecca Gilman was joint winner of the 1999 George Devine Award and won the 1999 Evening Standard Award for Most Promising Playwright for The Glory of Living.

Roy Williams and Gary Mitchell were joint winners of the George Devine Award 2000 for Most Promising Playwright for Lift Off and The Force of Change respectively. At the Barclays Theatre Awards 2000 presented by the TMA, Richard Wilson won the Best Director Award for David Gieselmann's Mr Kolpert and Jeremy Herbert won the Best Designer Award for Sarah Kane's 4.48 Psychosis. Gary Mitchell won the Evening Standard's Charles Wintour Award 2000 for Most Promising Playwright for The Force of Change. Stephen Jeffreys' I Just Stopped by to See The Man won an AT&T: On Stage Award 2000. David Eldridge's Under the Blue Sky won the Time Out Live Award 2001 for Best New Play in the West End. Leo Butler won the George Devine Award 2001 for Most Promising Playwright for Redundant. Roy Williams won the Evening Standard's Charles Wintour Award 2001 for Most Promising Playwright for Clubland. Grae Cleugh won the 2001 Olivier Award for Most Promising Playwright for Fucking Games.

In 1999, the Royal Court won the European theatre prize New Theatrical Realities, presented at Taormina Arte in Sicily, for its efforts in recent years in discovering and producing the work of young British dramatists.

ROYAL COURT BOOKSHOP

The bookshop offers a wide range of playtexts and theatre books, with over 1,000 titles. Located in the downstairs Bar and Food area, the bookshop is open Monday to Saturday, afternoons and evenings.

Many Royal Court playtexts are available for just £2 including works by Harold Pinter, Caryl Churchill, Rebecca Gilman, Martin Crimp, Sarah Kane, Conor McPherson, Ayub Khan-Din, Timberlake Wertenbaker and Roy Williams.

For information on titles and special events,
Email: bookshop@royalcourttheatre.com
Tel: 020 7565 5024

REBUILDING THE ROYAL COURT

In 1995, the Royal Court was awarded a National Lottery grant through the Arts Council of England, to pay for three quarters of a £26m project to completely rebuild its 100-year old home. The rules of the award required the Royal Court to raise £7.6m in partnership funding. The building has been completed thanks to the generous support of those listed below.

We are particularly grateful for the contributions of over 5,700 audience members.

English Stage Company Registered Charity number 231242.

ROYAL COURT DEVELOPMENT BOARD
Tamara Ingram (Chair)
Jonathan Cameron (Vice Chair)
Timothy Burrill
Anthony Burton
Jonathan Caplan QC
Deborah Davis
Cecily Engle
Kimberly Fortier
Julia Hobsbawm
Joyce Hytner
Mary Ellen Johnson
Dan Klein
Michael Potter
Mark Robinson
William Russell
Sue Stapely
James L Tanner

PRINCIPAL DONOR
Jerwood Foundation

WRITERS CIRCLE
The Cadogan Estate
Carillon/Schal
News International plc
Pathé
The Eva and Hans K Rausing Trust
The Rayne Foundation
Sky
Garfield Weston Foundation

DIRECTORS CIRCLE
The Esmée Fairbairn Foundation
The Granada Group plc

ACTORS CIRCLE
Edwin C Cohen & The Blessing Way Foundation
Sir Ronald Cohen & Sharon Harel-Cohen
Quercus Charitable Trust
The Basil Samuel Charitable Trust
The Trusthouse Charitable Foundation
The Woodward Charitable Trust

SPECIFIC DONATIONS
The Foundation for Sport and the Arts for Stage System
John Lewis Partnership plc for Balcony
City Parochial Foundation for Infra Red Induction Loops and Toilets for Disabled Patrons
RSA Art for Architecture Award Scheme for Antoni Malinowski Wall Painting

THE AMERICAN FRIENDS OF THE ROYAL COURT THEATRE

AFRCT support the mission of the Royal Court and are primarily focused on raising funds to enable the theatre to produce new work by emerging American writers. Since this not-for-profit organisation was founded in 1997, AFRCT has contributed to seven productions including Rebecca Gilman's Boy Gets Girl. They have also supported the participation of young artists in the Royal Court's acclaimed International Residency.

If you would like to support the ongoing work of the Royal Court, please contact the Development Department on 020 7565 5050.

AMERICAN FRIENDS

Founders
Harry Brown
Victoria Elenowitz
Francis Finlay
Monica Gerard-Sharp
The Howard Gilman Foundation
Jeananne Hauswald
Mary Ellen Johnson
Dany Khosrovani
Kay Koplovitz
The Laura Pels Foundation
The Magowan Family Foundation
Monica Menell-Kinberg Ph.D.
Benjamin Rauch
Rory Riggs
Robert Rosenkranz
Gerald Schoenfeld, The Shubert Organization

Patrons
Daniel Baudendistel
Arthur Bellinzoni
Miriam Bienstock
Robert L & Janice Billingsley
Catherine G Curran
Leni Darrow
Michael & Linda Donovan
Ursula & William Fairbairn
April Foley
Amanda Foreman
Mr & Mrs Richard Gelfond
Mr & Mrs Richard Grand
Mr & Mrs Paul Hallingby
Sharon King Hoge
The Carl C Icahn Family Foundation
Maurice & Jean R Jacobs
Mr & Mrs Ernest Kafka
Sahra T Lese
Susan & Martin Lipton
Eleanor Margolis
Hamish & Georgone Maxwell
Kathleen O'Grady
Howard & Barbara Sloan
Margaret Jackson Smith
Mika Sterling
Arielle Tepper
The Thorne Foundation

Benefactors
Mr & Mrs Tom Armstrong
Mr & Mrs Mark Arnold
Elaine Attias
Rachael Bail
Mr & Mrs Matthew Chapman
David Day
Richard & Rosalind Edelman
Abe & Florence Elenowitz
Hiram & Barbara Gordon
Mr & Mrs Brian Keelan
Jennifer C E Laing
Burt Lerner
Imelda Liddiard
Dr Anne Locksley
Mr & Mrs Rudolph Rauch
Lawrence & Helen Remmel
Mr & Mrs Robert Rosenberg
Mr & Mrs William Russell
Harold Sanditen
Mr & Mrs Robert Scully
Julie Talen
Mr & Mrs Charles Whitman

American Friends Development Director
Timothy Runion
Tel: (212) 408 0465

PROGRAMME SUPPORTERS

The Royal Court (English Stage Company Ltd) receives its principal funding from London Arts. It is also supported financially by a wide range of private companies and public bodies and earns the remainder of its income from the box office and its own trading activities.
The Royal Borough of Kensington & Chelsea gives an annual grant to the Royal Court Young Writers' Programme and the London Boroughs Grants Committee provides project funding for a number of play development initiatives.

The Jerwood Charitable Foundation continues to support new plays by new playwrights through the Jerwood New Playwrights series. Since 1993 the A.S.K. Theater Projects of Los Angeles has funded a Playwrights' Programme at the theatre. Bloomberg Mondays, the Royal Court's reduced price ticket scheme, is supported by Bloomberg.

TRUSTS AND FOUNDATIONS
American Friends of the Royal Court Theatre
Anon
The Carnegie United Kingdom Trust
Carlton Television Trust
Gerald Chapman Fund
The Foundation for Sport and the Arts
Genesis Foundation
The Goldsmiths' Company
Jerwood Charitable Foundation
John Lyon's Charity
The Laura Pels Foundation
Quercus Charitable Trust
The Peggy Ramsay Foundation
The Peter Jay Sharp Foundation
The Royal Victoria Hall Foundation
The Sobell Foundation
The Trusthouse Charitable Foundation
Garfield Weston Foundation

MAJOR SPONSORS
Amerada Hess
A.S.K. Theater Projects
AT&T: *OnStage*
BBC
Bloomberg
Channel Four
Royal College of Psychiatrists

BUSINESS MEMBERS
BP
CGNU plc
J Walter Thompson
Lazard
Lever Fabergé
McCABES
Pemberton Greenish
Peter Jones
Redwood
SIEMENS
Simons Muirhead & Burton

INDIVIDUAL MEMBERS
Patrons
Anon
Advanpress
Mark Bentley
Katie Bradford
Mrs Alan Campbell-Johnson
David Coppard
Chris Corbin
David Day
Mrs Phillip Donald
Thomas Fenton
Ralph A Fields
John Flower
Edna & Peter Goldstein
Homevale Ltd
Tamara Ingram
Mr & Mrs Jack Keenan
Barbara Minto
New Penny Productions Ltd
Martin Newson
AT Poeton & Son Ltd.
André Ptaszynski, Really Useful Theatres
Caroline Quentin
William & Hilary Russell
Ian & Carol Sellars
Miriam Stoppard
Carl & Martha Tack
Jan & Michael Topham
Mr & Mrs Anthony Weldon
Richard Wilson OBE
Amanda Vail

Benefactors
Anon
Anastasia Alexander
Lesley E Alexander
Mr & Mrs J Attard-Manché
Elaine Mitchell Attias
Matilde Attolico
Thomas Bendhem
Jasper Boersma
Keith & Helen Bolderson
Jeremy Bond
Brian Boylan
Mrs Elly Brook JP
Julian Brookstone
Paul & Ossi Burger
Debbi & Richard Burston
Yuen-Wei Chew
Martin Cliff
Carole & Neville Conrad
Conway Van Gelder
Coppard & Co.
Barry Cox
Curtis Brown Ltd
Peter Czernin
Deborah Davis
Chris & Jane Deering
Zöe Dominic
Robyn Durie
Lorraine Esdaile
Winston & Jean Fletcher
Nick Fraser
Jacqueline & Jonathan Gestetner
Michael Goddard
Carolyn Goldbart
Judy & Frank Grace
Byron Grote
Sue & Don Guiney
Hamilton Asper Management
Woodley Hapgood
Jan Harris
Phil Hobbs
Amanda Howard Associates
Mrs Martha Hummer-Bradley
Lisa Irwin-Burgess
Paul Kaju & Jane Peterson
Mr & Mrs T Kassem
Peter & Maria Kellner
Diana King
Clico Kingsbury
Lee & Thompson
Caroline & Robert Lee
Carole A Leng
Lady Lever
Colette & Peter Levy
Ann Lewis
Ian Mankin
Christopher Marcus
David Marks
Nicola McFarland
Mr & Mrs Roderick R McManigal
Mae Modiano
Eva Monley
Pat Morton
Georgia Oetker
Paul Oppenheimer
Janet & Michael Orr
Diana Parker
Maria Peacock
Pauline Pinder
Mr Thai Ping Wong
Jeremy Priestley
Simon Rebbechi
John & Rosemarie Reynolds
Samuel French Ltd
Bernice & Victor Sandelson
John Sandoe (Books) Ltd
Nicholas Selmes
Bernard Shapero
Jenny Sheridan
Lois Sieff OBE
Peregrine Simon
Brian D Smith
John Soderquist
The Spotlight
Max Stafford-Clark
Sue Stapely
June Summerill
Anthony Wigram
George & Moira Yip
Ms Tricia Young
Georgia Zaris

STAGE HANDS CIRCLE
Graham Billing
Andrew Cryer
Lindy Fletcher
Susan Hayden
Mr R Hopkins
Philip Hughes Trust
Dr A V Jones
Roger Jospe
Miss A Lind-Smith
Mr J Mills
Nevin Charitable Trust
Janet & Michael Orr
Jeremy Priestley
Ann Scurfield
Brian Smith
Harry Streets
Thai Ping Wong
Richard Wilson OBE
C C Wright

FOR THE ROYAL COURT

Royal Court Theatre, Sloane Square, London SW1W 8AS
Tel: 020 7565 5050 Fax: 020 7565 5001
info@royalcourttheatre.com
www.royalcourttheatre.com

ARTISTIC
Artistic Director **Ian Rickson**
Assistant to the Artistic Director **Jo Luke**
Associate Director **Dominic Cooke**
Associate Director International **Elyse Dodgson**
Associate Director Casting **Lisa Makin**
Associate Directors* **Stephen Daldry, James Macdonald, Katie Mitchell, Max Stafford-Clark, Richard Wilson**
Literary Manager **Graham Whybrow**
Literary Associate **Stephen Jeffreys** *
Voice Associate **Patsy Rodenburg***
Casting Assistant **Amy Ball**
International Administrator **Natalie Highwood**
International Associate **Ramin Gray**
International Assistant **Rachel Toogood**
Resident Dramatist **Roy Williams**

YOUNG WRITERS' PROGRAMME
Associate Director **Ola Animashawun**
Education Officer **Christine Hope**
Outreach Worker **Lucy Dunkerley**
Writers Tutor **Simon Stephens***
Administrative Assistant **Lorna Rees**

PRODUCTION
Production Manager **Paul Handley**
Deputy Production Manager **Sue Bird**
Facilities Manager **Fran McElroy**
Facilities Deputy **Adair Ballantine**
Production Assistant **Jane Ashfield**
Company Stage Manager **Cath Binks**
Head of Lighting **Johanna Town**
Lighting Deputy **Heidi Riley**
Assistant Electricians **Gavin Owen, Andrew Taylor**
Lighting Board Operator JTD **Richard Wright**
Head of Stage **Martin Riley**
Stage Deputy **Steven Stickler**
Stage Chargehand **Daniel Lockett**
Head of Sound **Paul Arditti**
Sound Deputy **Ian Dickinson**
Sound Operator JTD **Michael Winship** *
Head of Wardrobe **Iona Kenrick**
Wardrobe Deputy **Jackie Orton**

MANAGEMENT
Executive Director **Barbara Matthews**
Assistant to the Executive Director **Nia Janis**
General Manager **Diane Borger**
Administration Interns **Vanessa Cook, Juliette Goodman**
Finance Director **Sarah Preece**
Finance Officer **Rachel Harrison**
Finance Assistant **Martin Wheeler**
Accountant **Simone De Bruyker** *

MARKETING & PRESS
Head of Marketing **Penny Mills**
Head of Press **Ewan Thomson**
Marketing Officer **Charlotte Franklin**
Marketing and Press Assistant **Claire Christou**
Marketing Intern **Jennie Whitell**
Box Office Manager **Neil Grutchfield**
Deputy Box Office Manager **Valli Dakshinamurthi**
Duty Box Office Manager **Glen Bowman**
Box Office Sales Operators **Carol Pritchard, Steven Kuleshnyk**

DEVELOPMENT
Head of Development **Helen Salmon**
Development Associate **Susan Davenport** *
Sponsorship Manager **Rebecca Preston**
Development Officer **Alex Lawson**
Development Assistant **Chris James**
Development Intern **Vangel Efthimiadou**

FRONT OF HOUSE
Theatre Manager **Elizabeth Brown**
Deputy Theatre Manager **Jeremy Roberts**
Duty House Manager **Suzanne Kean, Paul McLaughlin, Neil Morris***
Bookshop Manager **Peggy Riley**
Assistant Bookshop Manager **Simon David**
Bookshop Assistants **Michael Chance, Jennie Fellows, Suzanne Kean**
Stage Door/Reception **Hannah Caughlin, Simon David, Kelda Holmes, Hannah Lawrence, Tyrone Lucas, Andrew Pepper, Kathleen Smiley**
Thanks to all of our ushers

* part-time

Martin Crimp

Face to the Wall
&
Fewer Emergencies

ff

faber and faber

First published in 2002
by Faber and Faber Limited
3 Queen Square, London WC1N 3AU

Typeset by Country Setting, Kingsdown, Kent CT14 8ES
Printed in England by Intype London Ltd

A CIP record for this book
is available from the British Library

ISBN 0-571-21625-0

2 4 6 8 10 9 7 5 3 1

Contents

FACE TO THE WALL

Four actors required
1, 2, 3 *and* **4**

Time

Blank

Place

Blank

/ indicates point of overlap in overlapping dialogue

1 Yes? says the receptionist, What can I do for you? How can I help you? Who did you want to see? Do you have an appointment?

2 He shoots her through the mouth.

1 He shoots her through the mouth and he goes down the corridor.

3 Quite quickly.

1 Goes——good——yes——quite quickly down the corridor——opens the first door he finds.

3 Walks straight in.

1 Walks straight in.

2 Yes? says the teacher, How can I help you?

1 Shoots him through the heart.

3 Shoots the teacher right through the heart.

1 The children don't understand——they don't immediately grasp what's going on——what's happened to their teacher?——they don't understand——nothing like this has ever / happened before.

3 Nothing like this has ever happened before——but they do understand——of course they understand——they've seen this on TV——they've stayed up late as a special treat and they've seen this on TV——they know exactly what's going on and this is why they back away——instinctively back away.

1 Okay——so they back away——the worst thing they could do——back away——but they back away——they back away against the wall.

2 Against their pictures on the wall——'My house'.

3 'My cat'.

2 'Me and my cat'.

3 'My house', 'Me and my cat', 'Me in a tree', and it's interesting to see the way that some of them / hold hands.

1 And it's interesting to see the way that some of them hold hands——they instinctively hold hands——the way children do——the way a child does——if you reach for its hand as it walks next to you it will grasp your own——not like an adult who will flinch away——never touch an adult's hand like this or the adult will flinch away——unless it's someone who loves you——a loved one——anyone else will flinch away——but a loved one will take your hand like a child——they will trust you like a child——a loved one won't flinch away——a loved one will hold your hand because the hand reminds you of your love——whole afternoons for example spent simply feeling the spaces between each other's fingers——or looking into the loved one's eyes——the thick rings of colour in the loved one's eyes——which are like something——what is it?——don't help me——the precipitate——the precipitate in a test tube——but anyone else——an adult——will flinch away——just as the child——child A——now flinches away from what?——yes?

4 From the warm metal.

1 From the warm metal——thank you——of the gun. Just as child A now flinches away from the warm metal of the gun. He shoots child A——in the head.

3 He moves on.

1 He moves on to child B. He shoots child B——in the head.

3 He moves on.

1 He moves on to child C. Child C——yes?

4 Tries to duck away.

1 What?

4 Child C tries / to duck away.

1 He shoots child B——in the head.

3 He moves on.

1 He moves on to child C. Child C tries to duck away. He shoots——no——yes——no——not shoots——yes?

4 But to no avail.

1 Tries to duck away. But to no avail. He shoots child A——in the head.

3 He moves on.

1 He moves on to child B. He shoots child B——in the head.

3 He moves on.

1 He moves on to child C. Child C tries to duck away. But to no avail. But to no avail. He shoots child C——good——in the head.

2 And how's life treating him?

1 What?

2 Life——how's life treating him?

1 Life's treating him very well.

3 How's his job?

1 His job is fine——well paid and rewarding.

3 And his wife?

1 Is charming and tolerant.

2 And how are his children?

1 His children are fine.

3 How many does he have now?

1 Four. He has four and all four of them are fine.

2 What? All four of them are fine?

1 All four——yes——is this right?——are absolutely fine. He loves swinging them through the air and hearing them scream with joy. When he gets back to their beautiful house he picks them off the ground and swings them screaming through the air.

3 And how is his beautiful house?

1 Increasing in value daily——well constructed and well located——close to amenities——schools——shops——major roads leading directly to major airports——minor roads——no——yes——minor roads——yes——minor roads winding——is it?——don't help me——don't help me——yes——minor roads winding through meadows watered by springs welling up through the chalk.

3 And how are the schools in his neighbourhood?

1 The schools in his neighbourhood are fine.

3 And the shops?

2 Yes——how's the shopping?

1 Excellent shopping——excellent——yes?

4 And not just the big names.

1 And not just the big names. Excellent shopping——excellent——and not just the big names but——yes?

4 Those kinds of / smaller shops.

1 Excellent shopping——excellent——and not just the big names but those kinds of smaller shops you thought——not thought——imagined?——yes?

4 You thought had all but / disappeared.

1 Disappeared. Excellent shopping——excellent——and not just the big names but those kinds of smaller shops you thought had all but disappeared.

3 I thought those smaller shops had all but disappeared.

1 Well yes they have——but not here——not here——here you can find all those kinds of smaller shops you thought had all but disappeared. He moves on.

2 What? Artisans?

1 Artisans——yes——people who bind books——people who make shoes——people who grind knives——people who mend rugs——people who gut fish——cut cheese——people who mix paint. He moves on.

3 Medical supplies?

1 Medical supplies——catering supplies——motoring supplies——yes?

4 Spare parts / for cars.

1 Spare parts for cars no longer manufactured but lovingly restored. He moves on. He shoots child D——in the head.

2 So there must be blood.

1 Well of course there's blood——not just blood on the wall——not just blood on the floor.

3 But blood in the air.

2 Blood in the air. Blood hanging in the air. A mist.

3 An aerosol.

1 An aerosol——that's right——that's good——of blood——which he hadn't foreseen——he hadn't foreseen the aerosol of blood——or the sound——is this right?——this is right——or the sound of the distressed children when his head was on the white pillow——on the white pillow——don't help me——when his head was on the white pillow picturing the scene——but now——don't help me——but now it's clear——now the picture is clear——and there's another sound——what's that other sound?——don't help me, don't help me——the sound of his heart——no——yes——yes——the sound of his heart——the sound of his own heart——the sound of the killer's heart sounding in the killer's head——that's right——that's good——which he hadn't foreseen——he hadn't foreseen the sound of his own heart in his own head——filling his head——his own heart filling his head with blood——popping his ears——popping his ears with blood——like a swimmer——not swimmer——don't help me——like a diver——this is right——diving into blood——he's like a diver diving into blood——that's right——that's good——very good——down he goes——down he goes away from the light——diving into blood——popping——popping his ears and what are you staring at?——eh?——eh?——what are you staring at?——turn away——look away——no——turn away——that's right——turn

away or you're next——be quiet or you're next——
that's right——that's good——you saw what
happened to child A, you saw what happened to
child B, you saw what happened to child C——you
saw what happened to child C——you saw what
happened to child C——no——yes——no——don't
help me——

Pause.

Don't help me——

4 You saw what happened to child D.

1 Don't help me——you saw what happened to child A, you saw what happened to child B, you saw what happened to child C, you saw what happened to child D, so——so——you saw what happened to child D, so——

4 So shut the / fuck up.

1 YOU SAW WHAT HAPPENED TO CHILD D, SO SHUT THE FUCK UP. CUNT. CUNT. LITTLE CUNT. I SAID DON'T HELP ME.

Long pause.

3 So he's not a sympathetic character.

1 No.

3 We can't feel for him.

1 No.

3 Cry for him.

1 No.

3 He's never suffered.

1 No.

3 Experienced war.

1 No.

3 Experienced poverty.

1 No.

2 Torture.

1 Torture?

2 Been tortured——yes——for his beliefs. You heard what / I said.

1 No. What beliefs? No.

2 Abused, then, as a child.

1 No.

2 Fucked up the arse as a child.

1 No.

3 Or in the mouth.

1 No.

2 Beaten.

3 Beaten by his dad breaking a leg off the chair in the kitchen. Beaten with a chair-leg.

1 No.

2 What about his own children?

3 Yes——perhaps they're sick.

1 No.

2 His wife?

3 His wife what?

2 Sick?

1 No.

2 Is his car unreliable?

1 No.

2 What about the milkman?

3 Yes——is the milkman in his neighbourhood ever late?

1 No.

2 Or the postman?

1 Sometimes.

Pause.

3 How does he feel when the postman's late?

1 Angry.

2 So now he's going to kill the postman.

3 Typical.

1 Of course he's not going to kill the postman. It's not the postman's fault——he knows it's not the postman's fault——sometimes there are problems sorting the letters——the machine for sorting the letters has broken down, for example, and the letters have to be sorted by hand——or perhaps there are lots of parcels and every parcel means a conversation on the doorstep.

Pause.

A conversation on the doorstep——yes?

4 In the sunshine.

1 Means a conversation on the doorstep in the sunshine. And sometimes the postman's boy can't wake the postman up. 'Dad, dad', he says 'it's five o'clock'——

4 'Wake up. It's five o'clock.'

1 'Dad, dad,' he says, 'Wake up. It's five o'clock. I've brought you / your tea.'

4 'Time to get up.'

1 What?

4 'Time / to get up.'

1 'Dad, dad,' he says, 'Wake up. It's five o'clock. Time to get up. I've brought you your tea.' But the postman——don't help me——but the postman——this is right——I'm right——don't help me——'Time to get up. I've brought you your tea.' But the postman——but the postman——but the postman just pushes himself harder against the wall.

*

Twelve-Bar Delivery Blues

Woke up this morning
Heard my son call
Turned away from the window
Turned my face to the wall.
Daddy daddy, he said to me
Daddy daddy, I've BROUGHT YOU YOUR TEA.

Son, I told him,
Your poor daddy's dead
There's another person
Come to live in his head.
Son son, your daddy's not well
Son son, your DADDY'S A SHELL.

There's another person
Speaking these lies
There's another person
Looking out through my eyes.
Son son, he's filing reports
Son son, he's PROMPTING MY THOUGHTS.

My son poured tea
From the brown china pot
Said, drink up your tea, dad,
Drink up while it's hot.
Daddy daddy, you're not sick at all
Daddy daddy, turn a-WAY FROM THE WALL.

Hey daddy,
You're a liar——and a fake
Take off those pyjamas
There's deliveries to make.
I lifted my head from my white pillow case
Threw my hot tea RIGHT IN HIS FACE.

Hey sonny,
If there's one thing I've learned
It's don't rub on butter
When your skin is all burned.
Son son, I ain't got no choice
Son son, I JUST HEAR THIS VOICE
(Saying . . .)

Doo ba ba-doo ba ba – Doo ba ba-doo ba ba –
Doo ba ba-doo ba ba – Doo ba ba-doo ba ba –
Doo ba ba-doo ba ba – Doo ba ba-doo ba ba –
Doo ba ba-doo ba ba – Doo ba ba-doo ba ba –
Doo ba ba-doo ba ba – Doo ba ba-doo ba ba –
Doo ba ba-doo ba ba – DOO DOO DOO DOO . . .

Woke up this morning
Heard my son call
Turned away from the window
Turned my face to the wall.
Son son, I hear what you say
But there just ain't gonna be no deliveries today . . .
(No way).

FEWER EMERGENCIES

Three actors required
1, 2 *and* 3

Time

Blank

Place

Blank

/ indicates point of overlap in overlapping dialogue

2 And how are things going?

1 Well things are improving. Things are improving day by day.

2 What kind of things?

1 Well, the light. The light is improving day by day.

2 Getting brighter?

1 What?

2 Getting brighter? Getting brighter day by day? Improving day by day? Getting brighter?

1 What?

2 Getting brighter? Getting brighter day by day? Improving.

1 Oh yes. Yes. Improving, yes. Getting brighter, yes.

2 Good.

1 Getting so much brighter, yes.

2 Good. I'm pleased.

1 I'm happy you're pleased.

2 I'm pleased about the light.

1 I'm pleased about the light too.

3 We're all pleased about the light.

2 Well, yes, of course we are——and are they still boating?

1 Both of them are still boating.

3 What? Gliding past?

1 Both of them are still gliding past when they get the chance, and they get the chance more and more often. More and more often they get the boat out——they set sail——they glide past in the boat.

3 So things are improving.

1 They're improving day by day. Not just the light, but boating too. They get the boat out——they check the supplies——they test the satellite telephone——they leave the estuary——and before you know it they're out on the ocean——slicing through the waves——travelling further and further afield.

3 More confidently.

1 Much more confidently.

2 How do they look?

1 Look?

3 Yes——good question——how do they look?

1 Well, confident——more confident.

3 You mean they're smiling? Or don't they need to smile?

2 They don't need to smile but they're smiling anyway.

3 What——in spite of themselves?

1 They're smiling——that's right——in spite of themselves. Or rather——no——correction——they

know they're smiling——but equally they know the kind of smile they're smiling resembles the kind of smile you smile in spite of yourself.

3 Say that again.

1 I can't say that again, but what I can say is that they still sing that little song.

2 They don't.

1 They do.

2 They don't.

1 They do, they do, they still sing that little song like something you hear in the supermarket.

3 Or in the DIY superstore, or on the porno film——when the swollen cock on the porno film goes into the swollen cunt.

2 So things are looking up.

1 Things are definitely looking up——brighter light——more frequent boating——more confident smile——things are improving day by day——who ever would've guessed?

2 Mmm?

1 Who ever would've guessed? Who ever would've thought the two of them could set sail like that towards the world's rim?

3 World's what?

1 World's rim. The rim of the world. The edge.

2 What edge? There is no edge of the world.

1 Oh yes there is. Oh yes there is an edge of the world.

2 Well, we won't argue.

1 We won't argue because there is an edge of the world——it's as simple as that. There's a rim like the rim of the plate, and past the rim is——what?

3 We don't know.

1 We don't know——it's as simple as that——we don't know what's past the / rim of the world.

2 So how are things looking when they leave the house?

1 Things are looking great. Things are improving. The whole neighbourhood is improving. The trees are more established, they've kicked out the Mexicans, they've kicked out the Serbs, people are finally cleaning up their own dog-mess, nice families are moving in.

2 Italians and Greeks?

3 Greeks, Italians, nice Chinese.

1 Nice Somalis, nice Chinese, really nice Kurds, really nice families who clean up their own dog-mess and hoover the insides of their cars. And what's more they've identified the gene——no——correction—— they've identified the sequence——that's right—— of genes that make people leave burnt mattresses outside their homes and strangled their babies.

2 Oh?

1 Yes——strangled their babies and installed better street lighting. Things are looking up. It's taken time of course. They've aged. Their hair's gone grey. But it doesn't stop them being desirable——far from it.

3 It doesn't stop them being desirable——it doesn't stop them boating——it doesn't stop them heading, like now, for the rim of the world——far from it—— or installing cupboards——

2 Far from it.

1 Far from it. It doesn't stop them installing cupboards for Bobby at the top of the spiral stairs——

3 Cupboards of precious wood.

1 Cupboards——that's right——of precious wood installed by joiners for all of Bobby's things——all the things Bobby will need in life for pleasure and for emergencies.

2 Candles?

1 Well naturally there are candles, boxes of matches, fresh figs, generators and barrels of oil. But there's also a shelf full of oak trees, and another where pine forests border a mountain lake. If you press a concealed knob a secret drawer pops open——inside is the island of Manhattan. And if you pull the drawers out, spilling the bone-handled knives and chickens onto the floor, spilling out the chain-saws and the harpsichords, there at the back, in the dark space at the back, is the city of Paris with a cloth over it to keep the dust out. There's a wardrobe full of uranium and another full of cobalt. Bobby's suits are hanging over a Japanese golf course. His shoes share boxes with cooked prawns. On one little shelf there's a row of universities——good ones——separated by restaurants where chefs are using the deep-fryers to melt gold and cast it into souvenir life-sized Parthenons. And hanging from the shelf, like the Beethoven quartets and fertility clinics, is the key, the key to use in emergencies, the key to get out of the house.

3 You mean he's locked in?

1 Well of course Jimmy's locked in——he's always locked in——he's locked in for his own protection.

2 Bobby.

1 What?

2 Bobby——not Jimmy——Bobby is locked in for his own protection.

1 I said Bobby.

2 You said Jimmy.

1 You think I don't know what I said?

2 Well we won't argue.

1 We won't argue because what I said was / Bobby.

3 What emergencies?

1 Oh, didn't I tell you?

3 What emergencies?

1 Oh, didn't I tell you? Because there's an emergency on right now. Rocks are being thrown——shots fired——that kind of stuff.

3 What? Cars are being overturned?

1 Cars are being——exactly——overturned and burnt.

2 Surely not Bobby's car?

1 Of course not Bobby's car——Bobby's not old enough to drive——but Bobby's neighbours' cars, Bobby's friends' cars, Bobby's parents' cars——yes——of course——are being first turned on their sides, then completely overturned, and burnt.

2 I thought things were improving.

1 Things *are* improving——less rocks are thrown——less cars completely overturned——less shots fired——there are fewer emergencies than there used to be——but all the same, there's an emergency on right now. It's on right now. And I'm sorry to say that one of

those shots came through the kitchen window and caught poor Bobby in the hip.

2 Oh?

1 Yes——I'm afraid so——it caught poor Bobby in the hip which is why instead of running up those stairs, he's——what?

3 He's crawling?

1 He's crawling——that's right——that's good——up the spiral stairs. Using his arms mainly.

2 He wants to reach the key.

1 He wants to open the door.

2 He must be mad.

3 Open the door? He must be / completely mad.

1 Ah yes——but you have to know what's going on in Bobby's mind. In Bobby's mind, if he opens the door, if he lets people in, if he takes them up the stairs, shows them the cupboards of precious wood, the fresh figs, the knives and the uranium——if he lifts a corner of the cloth and gives them a glimpse of Paris——if he shows them the swollen cock going into the swollen cunt and lets them pick a restaurant or a string quartet——if, after a swim in the mountain lake, he lets them take home a human egg——then what?——they'll what?——they'll . . . Yes?

3 Love him.

2 They'll love him

1 Then they'll always love him.

Pause.

Exactly.

3 Ship to shore.

1 What?

3 Ship to shore. They're calling him from the boat. They're calling him from the rim of the world on the satellite telephone. 'Bobby? Are you there?'

2 He's not answering.

1 Well of course he's not answering. He's pulling himself up the spiral stairs. He wants to get / to the key.

3 'Pick up the phone, Bobby.'

1 He's got the hang of it now: pull with the arms—— let the legs drag——concentrate.

2 So things are looking up.

3 Things are definitely looking up——more efficient use of his arms——more understanding of the geometry of the stairs——improved / concentration.

1 Brighter light——more frequent boating——more confident smile——fewer / emergencies.

2 It doesn't worry them then?

1 What?

2 It doesn't worry them that Bobby's not answering.

1 Of course it worries them——that's why they smile——that's why they sing that little song.

2 They don't.

1 They do.

2 They don't.

1 They do, they do——they push their grey hair out of their bright grey eyes and sing that little song.

3 (*sings – very soft and relaxed scat-singing*)
Doo doo-ba-dee doo doo doo ba-doo . . .
Ba doo-ba-dee doo, ba doo-ba dee doo . . .

Say ten seconds of this. Then slight pause. Then the others join in in unison, singing longer and more intense phrases. The lights begin a slow fade, reaching black where indicated.

1, 2, 3
Doo doo-ba-dee doo doo doo ba-doo . . .
Ba doo-ba-dee doo, ba doo-ba dee doo . . .
Ba doo-ba doo doo doo-ba doo-ba dee doo . . .

Maybe twenty-five seconds of this. Then pause. Lights still fading.

3 And Bobby?

1 Mmm?

3 And Bobby?

1 What he's losing in blood he's gaining in confidence. Light's flaring through the windows——flames—— it's getting brighter——he can see the key——

Black.

2 Things are improving.

1 Things are improving. He's further up the stairs. He's closer to the key. See how it spins——no—— correction——swings——see how / it swings.

2 See how the key swings.

3 That's right, Bobby-boy. Watch the key. Watch the key swinging.

10 September 2001